Contents

Sleeping

Sleeping is what you do when you go to bed. When you are asleep, you stay mostly still and quiet and you breathe more slowly, too.

You close your eyes as you go to sleep.

Healthy Habits

Sleep and rest

Sue Barraclough

W

FRANKLIN WATTS
LONDON • SYDNEY

This edition 2013

First published in 2010 by
Franklin Watts
338 Euston Road
London NW1 3BH

Franklin Watts Australia
Level 17/207 Kent Street
Sydney NSW 2000

Series editor: Julia Bird
Design: Jane Hawkins
Art director: Jonathan Hair

A CIP catalogue record for this book is available from the British Library.

ISBN 978 1 4451 1728 7
Dewey classification: 591.5'19

Picture credits: Banana Stock/Jupiter Images/Getty Images: 22; Adrian Burke/Corbis: 21;
Corbis Edge/Corbis: 1, 11, 12; Adrian Davies/Nature PL: 15; Silke Dietze/istockphoto: 7;
Karin Dreyer/Blend/Corbis: 20; Brooke Fasani/Corbis: front cover t; Flirt/Corbis: 4;
Kim Gunkel/istockphoto: 8; Adrian Hepworth/NHPA: front cover b, 5; Image 100/Corbis: 14;
Move Art Management/Corbis: 16; Owen Newman/Nature PL: 2, 6; Rolf Nussbaumer/Nature PL: 17;
Pixland/Jupiter Images/Getty Images: 18; Philippe Psaila/SPL: 10 H. Reinhard/Arco Images/Alamy: 9;
Cyril Ruoso/Minden Pictures/ FLPA: 13; John Tomaselli/istockphoto: 23;
Shin Yoshino/Minden Pictures/FLPA: 19.

Every attempt has been made to clear copyright.
Should there be any inadvertent omission,
please apply to the publisher for rectification.

Printed in China

Franklin Watts is a division of Hachette Children's Books,
an Hachette UK company.
www.hachette.co.uk

Humans and other animals need to sleep.
We need sleep to stay **healthy**.

Most birds sleep
with the head turned
and resting on the
shoulder.

Resting

Resting means **relaxing** your body because you are tired. **Active** animals need rest to keep their bodies fit and healthy. Animals need to be fit and healthy so they can find food or escape **predators**.

This jaguar is resting, but it can move fast if it needs to!

Sometimes when you have been playing and running, your body feels tired. Sitting or lying down for a short rest can help you to feel more active again.

Think about it

How does your body feel when you have been running?

Sleep and staying well

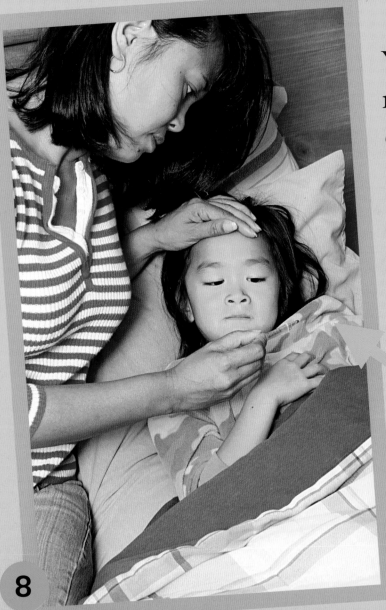

Your body grows and **repairs** itself while you are asleep. When you are ill, your body needs even more sleep so that you can get well again quickly.

Sleep and rest makes a body stronger and more able to fight off illness.

Think about it

Have you ever been ill or injured and had to stay in bed?

Animals that have been hurt need to rest their bodies, too. In time, a body part can often repair itself.

Babies and sleep

Young animals need to spend a lot of time sleeping and resting to grow and stay healthy. Mothers often carry their sleeping babies to keep them safe.

A sleeping baby lemur clings tightly to its mother as it sleeps.

Q Which animal sleeps the most?

A The brown bat. It can sleep for up to 20 hours a day!

Babies and children's bodies grow and change as they sleep. A baby may sleep for most of the day as well as at night.

Babies and children need more sleep than adults.

11

Beds and nests

You sleep in a bed at night. You have pyjamas and covers to keep you warm.

Think about it

How do you feel when you are in your bed?

Chimpanzees make a new nest every night.

Chimpanzees make a nest of leaves and branches to sleep in. Each chimpanzee finds a safe place in a tree to build a nest.

13

Feeling sleepy

Sometimes you may feel sleepy during the day. Feeling sleepy often means that your body and **brain** need to rest.

Think about it

How do you feel when you do not have enough sleep?

Sitting still for a long time can make you sleepy.

Yawning can mean that you are sleepy. All animals yawn from time to time. Other clues that you are tired are blinking, a nodding head and heavy arms and legs.

Light and dark

Most people sleep better in a dark room. Light tells your brain to wake up. Going to bed and waking up at the same time every day helps you to have a good **sleep pattern**.

You wake up in the morning when it is light.

Many animals move around to hunt or to find food at night. These animals sleep or rest during the day.

Why are many desert animals active at night?

Deserts are hot places, so many animals come out at night when it is cooler.

An owl comes out at night to hunt.

Waking up

When you first wake up, your body may feel slow and heavy. It can take a while for your brain and body to get active again.

Animals often **stretch** their bodies when they wake up. This helps to get the body moving after staying still.

This cheetah stretches its legs before it moves.

Think about it

How do you feel when you wake up?

Sleep and dream

Your brain is active even while you sleep. While you sleep you may **dream**. Dreaming can help you to learn and remember things.

You only dream for part of the time that you are asleep.

Think about it

Can you remember what you dreamed about last night?

You may have seen a cat or dog dreaming. Sometimes their eyes twitch and their feet move as if they are dreaming about running.

Tips for healthy sleep

✓ Sleep in a dark, **comfortable** room that is not too hot or too cold. Have a night-light if you need one.

✓ Go to bed and wake up at the same time each day. This helps you to have a healthy sleep pattern.

✓ Try to be active for at least one hour each day. This will help you sleep well.

✓ If you have a problem sleeping, talk to your parents.

A night light can help if you do not like your bedroom to be too dark.

✘ Do not exercise just before bedtime. It will make your body and brain too active.

✘ Do not eat a big meal just before bedtime. You will not sleep well.

✘ Do not drink a big glass of water just before bedtime. You will probably have to wake up in the night to go to the toilet.

You need to drink lots of water to be healthy, but avoid it for an hour or so before bedtime!

Glossary

active ready to move and do something.
brain the organ in your head that helps you to think, feel and move.
comfortable something that makes you feel relaxed.
dream feel and see things in your mind as you sleep.
healthy strong and full of energy.
predator an animal that kills and eats other animals.
relax make your body less stiff.
repair to fix something that is broken or hurt.
sleep pattern how long and well you usually sleep.
stretch make something straighter and longer.

Index

24